A Hope That Does Not Disappoint

Second Lesson Sermons For
Sundays After Pentecost (First Third)
Cycle C

Billy D. Strayhorn

CSS Publishing Company, Inc., Lima, Ohio

A HOPE THAT DOES NOT DISAPPOINT

Copyright © 2000 by
CSS Publishing Company, Inc.
Lima, Ohio

All rights reserved. No part of this publication may be reproduced in any manner whatsoever without the prior permission of the publisher, except in the case of brief quotations embodied in critical articles and reviews. Inquiries should be addressed to: Permissions, CSS Publishing Company, Inc., P.O. Box 4503, Lima, Ohio 45802-4503.

Some scripture quotations are from the *New Revised Standard Version of the Bible,* copyright 1989 by the Division of Christian Education of the National Council of the Churches of Christ in the USA. Used by permission.

Library of Congress Cataloging-in-Publication Data

Strayhorn, Billy D., 1951-
   A hope that does not disappoint : second lesson sermons for Sundays after Pentecost (first third) Cycle C / Billy D. Strayhorn.
     p. cm.
   ISBN 0-7880-1749-7 (alk. paper)
   1. Pentecost season—Sermons. 2. Bible. N.T. Epistles of Paul—Sermons. 3. Sermons—American. 4. Lectionary preaching. I. Title.
BV4300.5 .S75   2000
252'.64—dc21   00-036195
                                                                                              CIP

This book is available in the following formats, listed by ISBN:
   0-7880-1749-7   Book
   0-7880-1750-0   Disk
   0-7880-1751-9   Sermon Prep

For more information about CSS Publishing Company resources, visit our website at www.csspub.com.

PRINTED IN U.S.A.

I would like to dedicate this book to two people. First, to the memory of my first pastor, the Reverend Robert W. Core. My mentor and friend, he introduced me to a deeper relationship with Christ and saw in me the makings of a minister. Bob, words will never express what that introduction has meant to my life.

And second, I dedicate this book to my wife, Mary. She's the real preacher in the family. In the first few years of our marriage, she showed me what the Christian life was all about by living it day to day. There was a quality to her life that I realized I was missing. Because of her, I began searching for it. Mary bought me my first Bible to help in that search. That lead to worship and much much more. Because of her, it stuck. Thanks for making it stick and for sticking with me.

Acknowledgments

There are so many people to thank and acknowledge. My family and everyone who ever encouraged me in this endeavor. To everyone in my Wednesday morning breakfast group and to the colleagues in my clergy support group: thanks for your prayers. Thanks to all the churches over the years who have put up with my preaching. Thanks to CSS Publishing for asking me to submit material and helping me fulfill a lifelong dream.

I would like to thank Kay Laws and Pat Selby for their invaluable help during the last two weeks of writing. They provided me with both time and humor during the creative process. Finally, I would especially like to thank Pat who spent hours reading and helping me make corrections.

Table Of Contents

Introduction   7

Pentecost   9
   Bewitched, Bothered, And Bewildered
   Acts 2:1-21

Holy Trinity   15
   A Hope That Does Not Disappoint
   Romans 5:1-5

Corpus Christi   23
   Our Daily Bread
   1 Corinthians 11:23-26

Proper 4   29
Pentecost 2
Ordinary Time 9
   We Are Witnesses
   Galatians 1:1-12

Proper 5   39
Pentecost 3
Ordinary Time 10
   Born And Called
   Galatians 1:11-24

Proper 6   47
Pentecost 4
Ordinary Time 11
   By Faith In Christ
   Galatians 2:15-21

Proper 7   53
Pentecost 5
Ordinary Time 12
    Heirs According To The Promise
    Galatians 3:23-29

Proper 8   59
Pentecost 6
Ordinary Time 13
    Life In The Spirit
    Galatians 5:1, 13-25

Proper 9   65
Pentecost 7
Ordinary Time 14
    Bear One Another's Burdens
    Galatians 6:(1-6) 7-16

Proper 10   73
Pentecost 8
Ordinary Time 15
    Get Your Transfer Here
    Colossians 1:1-14

Lectionary Preaching After Pentecost   79

Introduction

This book consists of sermons preached or prepared for the period of year beginning with the celebration of Pentecost and the Sundays which follow. Pentecost is the birthday of the church. Pentecost was the day the hopes and dreams of the disciples and followers of Jesus began to take shape. Pentecost was the day the Holy Spirit blew into town and set the hearts and lives of the disciples and followers of Jesus on fire.

Just as the church began on Pentecost, this book begins there, too. It was through the presence and power of the Holy Spirit that the Church took shape and the Good News spread. It is through the presence and power of the Holy Spirit that we find the mission and challenge of the Church today. It is through the presence and power of the Holy Spirit that we are still given the strength, purpose, and power to carry out God's mission.

And most importantly, it is through the presence and power of the Holy Spirit that we find hope — hope for tomorrow and hope for today. It is through the presence and power of the Holy Spirit that Paul reminds us, if that hope is founded and built upon Christ, then it will be a "hope that does not disappoint."

In a world filled with disappointments we need this "hope that does not disappoint."

Pentecost

Bewitched, Bothered, And Bewildered

Acts 2:1-21

A farm family had some friends from the city come to visit. The friends had a young boy who had never experienced life on a farm. To make his visit somewhat more memorable, the hostess took the little boy with her out to the henhouse when she went to gather eggs. The little boy was puzzled by what he saw, because on the way out of the henhouse he asked, "Why do you keep your eggs out here? My mom keeps hers in the refrigerator!"

Just like that little boy, the observers at the first Pentecost were a little puzzled by what was going on.

Today is Pentecost Sunday, the day we celebrate as the birthday of the Church. This is the day on which the promised Counselor and Comforter, the Holy Spirit, touched and filled and changed the lives of the disciples. Pentecost is the day we celebrate the Promise, the Power, and the Purpose of God's Holy Spirit.

The Promise

Old Blue Eyes, the Chairman of the Board, Frank Sinatra passed away. He had a wonderfully smooth and mellow voice. I know a man who grew up listening to Frank Sinatra and the others in the Rat Pack — Dean Martin and Sammy Davis, Jr. Not by choice mind you. His taste in music was more in the sounds of Eric Clapton, Stevie Ray Vaughn, and Jimi Hendrix, but his mother loved Frank Sinatra and she would listen to him and the others all the time, especially when she was cleaning house. As boys, this man and his brothers always had to help. Mom would slap on five or six Frank Sinatra and Dean Martin albums (does anybody remember those?), crank up the stereo so she could hear it all over the house, and go to town cleaning and singing. This man says he heard those records so many times he could sing along with almost all of Frank Sinatra's songs. Songs like: "Strangers In The Night," "In The Wee Small Hours Of the Morning," "Young At Heart," "Chicago, My Kind Of Town," "High Hopes," "My Way," and "Bewitched, Bothered, and Bewildered."

That last song, "Bewitched, Bothered, and Bewildered," might come to mind as you read about that first Pentecost. The crowd who witnessed it was certainly bothered and bewildered by all they witnessed. And they couldn't explain what was going on, so they accused the disciples of being drunk or bewitched. But they were wrong. The disciples were neither drunk nor bewitched. They were simply filled with the promise fulfilled.

At the Last Supper and at his Ascension, Jesus promised that the Holy Spirit would come and fill the disciples. Jesus promised that the Spirit would fill them and remind them of all he had taught them. And Jesus promised they would be filled with both power and purpose.

Until the day of Pentecost that promise laid there like an uninflated balloon. You see an uninflated balloon is still a balloon but it is really more the promise of a balloon than it is a balloon. It's not really a balloon until it is blown up or filled with helium or water. Until then it is only the promise of what it can be. But once it's filled full, then the promise is fulfilled.

Pentecost was the day the promise was fulfilled and the disciples were filled full of the Holy Spirit. It was the day their promise received power and purpose.

The Power

The events of Pentecost gave birth to the Church. We celebrate birthdays and joke about certain ages but some people don't like birthdays because they don't like the prospect of getting older. You all have probably seen the list going around the Internet titled, "You Know You're Getting Older When...." Let me remind you of just a few.

You know you're getting older:
When you know all the answers but nobody is asking you any questions.
When you can sit in the rocking chair but can't get it going.
When all the names in your little black book end with M.D.
When your knees buckle and your belt won't.
When you get winded playing chess.
When you try to straighten the wrinkles in your socks and realize that you aren't wearing any.
When you stop halfway up the stairs and can't remember if you're going up or coming down.
When the first thing you hear in the morning is snap, crackle, and pop, and it's not cereal.
When it takes twice as long to recover from acting half your age. Then you know you're getting old.

The Church is nearly 2,000 years old. Sometimes it limps along like it's close to death. Sometimes it has the energy and excitement of a newborn. But when it was first born God threw a party called Pentecost. And when you throw a birthday party you usually bring gifts, right? Well, God didn't forget; the gift was the Holy Spirit.

Scripture describes that gift coming like this: "Suddenly from heaven there came a sound like the rush of a violent wind." The disciples heard the Spirit coming.

Most churches have a lot of coffee drinkers. Coffee drinkers often listen to the sucking in of air sound that happens when you open up a can of coffee. Some people think that sound is comforting. To them, it's like the sound of gravel under the tires of your vehicle; it's a wonderful sound, a comforting sound.

That unique sound from coffee comes from the fact that coffee is vacuum packed. All the air is pumped out and the can is sealed. When you break the seal with a can opener, the air rushes in to fill the void. Up to this point, in the life of the disciples, there was a void. Jesus was gone. They had seen him ascend into heaven. And they were alone. There was something missing in their lives. Then suddenly that void was filled. God sent the Holy Spirit and it rushed in with the sound of a mighty wind to fill that void. It rushed in with the power of God to fill them full of God's purpose.

The Purpose

The purpose of this in-rushing was to empower the disciples and the early Church to proclaim the Good News to all the world. A portion of this passage sounds as if Rand McNally or one of the other mapping companies wrote it, doesn't it? We have a list of folks from nearly every known part of the world. They spoke as many different languages as there were people present. Yet, when the disciples stood up to preach and bear witness to the Good News of Jesus Christ, every one of those divergent people heard the Good News in his or her own language.

The effects of the Tower of Babel had suddenly been reversed. Remember that incident from Genesis? In its pride, humanity decided to make a name for itself and build a tower all the way to heaven. But God didn't like that idea. God destroyed the tower and created the different languages so we couldn't communicate as readily and do something like that again.

Pentecost changed all that, at least for that day and that moment. Through the power of God's Holy Spirit, everyone that day heard and understood the Good News of Jesus Christ. Now it *was* a little odd. Most of the guys who were doing the talking were from Galilee. And Galilee was seen as that little backwater district. Galileans were seen as country bumpkins, or "Rednecks" as comedian Jeff Foxworthy calls them.

So, it was a little weird for all these foreigners to be hearing these Galileans preach in their native language. It was sort of like hearing Jeff Foxworthy speaking fluent French or the Three Stooges speaking Latin, Greek, and Arabic. It was odd, but God had a purpose. And that purpose was the spreading of the Good News. Each person there heard the message of the Good News of Jesus Christ in his or her own language. They heard and they understood.

There was a little girl who had the opportunity to meet a little German girl her own age. All afternoon they ran, chased butterflies, played tag, and played dolls together. Her parents were awestruck at how well these two little girls got along, in spite of the fact that neither spoke a word of the other's language. Later when Mom asked, "Could you understand anything the German girl said to you?" the little girl said, "No!"

Mom asked, "Did she understand you?"

Her daughter shook her head and said, "No, she didn't."

"But you played so well together. How..?"

"Oh, Mommy," the little girl exclaimed, "we understood each other's giggles!"

Language doesn't have to be a barrier, especially when the Holy Spirit is involved. God took the last barrier down. On Pentecost they all heard and they all understood — which meant they could all go back to their own country and share the Good News of the Resurrection of Christ from the dead: the forgiveness of sins and the new life in Christ with others.

The Promise was fulfilled. The disciples were filled full of God's Power so they could fulfill God's Purpose. The Holy Spirit, this birthday present from God, is really God with us, the Spirit of God and the Spirit of Christ with us always. Revelation 21:3 is fulfilled. "See, the home of God is among mortals. He will dwell with them as their God; they will be his peoples, and God himself will be with them."

Our challenge is to let the promise, the power, and the purpose of God's Holy Spirit fill our lives just as it filled the lives of the disciples on that first Pentecost.

Holy Trinity

A Hope That Does Not Disappoint

Romans 5:1-5

Rain or shine, hot or cold, seven nights a week, 365 days a year, members of area local churches and synagogues gather to bring hope to some 100 men, women, and children at the Arlington Night Shelter in Arlington, Texas. Volunteers check in people who are facing some of the hardest struggles in life. The volunteers greet the clients with a smile and help them get their few belongings settled. The clients are assigned chores like cleaning bathrooms, taking out trash, cleaning the living rooms, and doing laundry. Everyone takes some responsibility when they stay.

Clients sign up for washing machines so they can do their own laundry. It is important to look your best when you go to work or when you go for a job interview. Clients check out towels and washcloths and are given soap and shampoo. (One of the volunteers who travels extensively collects all the complimentary soaps and shampoos from his hotel rooms and donates them to the shelter.)

After check in, the clients visit with the social workers about any skills classes they should take and about personal issues. The next day's schedules are posted. All clients are expected to seek guidance and be actively seeking employment. The Night Shelter provides temporary help and assistance, leading its clients to independence.

Clients are given a hot meal each night. Volunteers prepare and serve these meals. It takes a lot of food to feed 100 people. Meals for those who are working late are prepared and set back so that all clients get fed. Most come back for seconds. Occasionally one or two will ask for third or fourth helpings. One night a little girl had six heaping-helpings of corn, her favorite. Like the miracle of the loaves and fishes, there is always more than enough.

Every night the population of the shelter changes as do the faces of those serving them. But one thing never changes, the hope and love brought and shared. For many of these temporary residents, Arlington Night Shelter is the first and only glimpse of hope they have ever had. And they find it "a hope that does not disappoint."

Here in Romans, Paul talks about "a hope that does not disappoint"; a hope that springs up even in the midst of suffering. How can that be? How can there be hope in the midst of a seemingly hopeless situation? From where does that hope come?

Paul paints a beautiful picture of hope born of our Trinitarian faith. With deft brush strokes, Paul paints a peaceful pastoral filled with bold splashes of glory in the midst of dark wide strokes of suffering. The peace and hope of this painting are not merely overlaid as an afterthought, they are an integral part of the painting. The brush strokes contain the dull colors of suffering and the muted colors of endurance, all suffused with the warm glow of hope. And like the paintings of the Impressionists who painted with little dots of paint, you can't see the fullness of the painting until you step back. One rarely sees the hope in the midst of the suffering. But, as Paul reminds us so deftly, it *is* there, just as it is everywhere in life. How do we come to know and experience that hope?

Peace With God

First, as Paul says, our hope comes through Peace with God. And that's good because life is full of trouble and adversity. We wish it were different but the truth is we never know when life is going to throw us an unexpected curve.

A police officer stopped a man for driving a truck with a broken taillight. The driver walked to the back of his car, looked at the burned out taillight, and then became very distressed. The officer tried to console the man, "Don't take it so hard, buddy; it's just a minor offense."

"That's not what's bothering me," replied the driver. "What's really bothering me is what happened to my wife and my trailer?"

Life is full of troubles and adversity. You can be cruising along, and everything seems to be going great. Life is good. God is in heaven and all is right with the world. It's so good you've got it on cruise control. Then all of a sudden you find yourself in a sideways slide or a head-over-tail flip and you can't figure out how you got there.

At times, some folks seem to be in the wrong place at the wrong time. Life just randomly reaches up and slaps them. There is no good or bad reason for it. It just happens. They find themselves suddenly out of a job, they are diagnosed with cancer, or there is the death of a loved one in their family. There is no forewarning and nothing to signal the onslaught of tragedy. It just happens.

But sometimes, probably most of the time, we bring that curve on ourselves. We live a lifestyle of overindulgence which contributes, if not causes, heart disease. We don't pay attention when we're driving, juggling our laptop and our cell phone and adjusting the radio all at the same time. Or we put our marriage and family on cruise control while we work like a dog at our job, trying to get that promotion. We neglect those who need us the most and whom we need the most. All of these things are tragedies just waiting to happen.

We do the same thing in our relationship with God. We don't take time for prayer or study. We skip worship one week to play golf with the guys or to go fishing or whatever. One week leads to another. We take God for granted. Then one day we look up. We find that we're so far away from God that we're not sure God will even recognize us when we do come back.

Or maybe we've never really had a relationship with God. We look at our lives and we realize we have anything but peace with God.

The Good News is that God does not forget us. God does not desert us. We may desert God, we may turn away, we may break covenant and think we are at odds with God. The Good News is we *can* have peace with God. That is God's desire for us. God, the creator and author of all that is, desires to have a personal relationship with us. God wants us to be part of the family. God wants us all to have equal access to the promises of the kingdom, through Christ Jesus.

There isn't some long drawn-out initiation process we are required to go through. There's no hazing. We can't be blackballed. There isn't a stack of forms and applications we have to weed our way through and answer correctly.

There is no twenty-question quiz. There is no thirty-page essay question we have to answer. We don't need to memorize the books of the Bible in proper order. We don't have to be able to spout off the names of the prophets and identify which are the minor and which are the major prophets.

It's not like a ride at an amusement park, we don't have to be a certain height to get on this ride of faith. We don't need a chaperone. We don't need a date. There is not an entrance fee. It's not like applying for a job; we don't need a resume.

Access To Grace

So, how do we get in? What's the secret word? What's the password? How do we have this personal relationship that can bring peace with God?

The answer is quite simple. We have obtained access to the grace of God through Jesus. The only letter of recommendation that we need is the one Christ Jesus gives for all. We don't need any other references but his. His signature, his Word, his nail-scarred hands are all we need. He is our letter of introduction, our entrance fee, our resume, and letter of recommendation. He is all we need. All we need to do is have faith in him. All we need to do is trust in the grace of God through Christ.

Have you ever tried something because of someone else's recommendation? Maybe it was a movie. You read a review or talked to some friends who had seen it before you. They liked it. They raved about it. You've known this couple for years and they have never lead you astray. Your movie tastes are very similar. So, in an act of trust, you go see that particular movie, trusting that you will like it at least as much as they did.

Or maybe it wasn't a movie. Maybe it was a restaurant. A certain friend recommended a new restaurant so you loaded up the family and went to try it.

It could be any number of things, a furniture store, a book, a Bible study, software, a recipe, gadgets, a babysitter, a car dealer, a new brand of soap, a magazine, or whatever. We all have tried something because of someone else's recommendation. Most of the time we weren't disappointed. Our friends and family were right.

We have been given access to the Grace of God in a similar way. We have been given access to the Grace of God through God's only Son, Jesus the Christ. In a sense, through Paul's letter and the Gospels, Christ is recommended to us. But at the same time, we who have drifted away from God, we who have turned and walked away, we who have sought our own selfish way in life need someone to stand up for us. We need someone to intervene. We need someone to write a letter of recommendation. We need Jesus. Jesus is our letter of recommendation. Scripture recommends him to us and he recommends us to God.

Years ago I read or heard about a pastor during the American Revolution who was a friend of George Washington. In this pastor's hometown there was a man who was one of those thorns in the flesh. This gentleman did just about everything he could think of to oppose and humiliate that pastor. One day the troublemaker was arrested for treason and sentenced to die.

You would think this pastor would have been relieved. But instead he traveled over seventy miles on foot to Philadelphia to plead with General Washington for the life of this traitor. After Washington heard his plea, he said, "No, I'm sorry. I cannot grant you the life of your friend."

"My friend!" exclaimed the old preacher. "He's the worst enemy I have."

Washington was astounded. "You've walked seventy miles to save the life of an enemy? That puts it all in a different light. I'll grant your pardon." And he did. That pastor walked home with the man who had deviled his life for so long. Only it was a journey of friends, not enemies.

We don't need any other recommendation but Christ's. His word and his nail-scarred hands are all we need. Through Christ we have access to the grace of forgiveness, the grace of new life, the grace of friendship and peace with God.

Hope Through The Spirit

Midnight the wonder dog is half Labrador retriever and half coonhound. She's called Midnight because she is black. She's called "the wonder dog" partly because of the tricks she can do and partly because sometimes her owners wonder why they have her. Midnight loves it when her owners rent movies from the local video store. You have never seen a dog wiggle and dance and get excited like Midnight does when her owners bring home a movie. When that movie finally gets popped into the VCR the excitement dies down and Midnight goes into wait mode. She sits through the whole movie, waiting and watching, not the movie but the plastic container the video tapes are transported in.

Midnight watches and listens with hope and expectation. When the movie is over and the tape is ejected, Midnight begins to get excited. She knows that sound. She knows what it means. You can see the anticipation in her eyes. Her ears go up in attentive mode. And when the tape is put in the re-winder, Midnight gets wound up. She knows what is coming soon, if not next. When the re-winder gets finished rewinding and the tape pops up, so does Midnight. Sometimes she even barks her approval and excitement.

And when her owners put the tape back in its plastic container, Midnight can no longer contain herself. She starts bouncing in excitement, bouncing in anticipation, waiting and hoping to hear the right words. Those words? "Come on, Midnight. Let's go for a ride. Let's take the movie back."

At the sound of those words, all of her hope, anticipation, and expectation come to fruition. She gets to go for a ride, one of her favorite things in all of the known dog world. She can hardly contain herself. If the keys don't come out immediately, she starts barking with impatience. She has waited long enough. It's doggie heaven when the garage door opens, the door of the vehicle is opened, and she enters and sits in her seat, ready to go for a ride. It doesn't make any difference to her that the video store is only a couple of blocks away. She is going for a ride. It doesn't make any difference to her that she won't be able to get out and run around. She is going for a ride. It doesn't make any difference to her that she has no idea what a movie really is. She is taking the movie back and she is going for a ride.

All of this excitement and anticipation, all of this hope is caused by a video tape and the plastic box it comes in. But more importantly it is caused by a hope that does not disappoint. Midnight knows from experience that if a movie comes into the house, then at some time, it has to go back and she will probably get to go for a ride and help take it back. Her hope is not disappointed.

We could say the same thing about the hope we receive from God through God's Holy Spirit.

Hope that comes through the Holy Spirit does not disappoint. It comes as a reminder that we are forgiven. The Spirit reminds us of the burden we once bore, the burden of our sins. And the Spirit reminds us how relieved we were when that burden was lifted.

The Spirit reminds us that we belong to God and nothing can separate us from God. And that fills us with hope, a hope that does not and will not disappoint.

And with that hope we can endure almost anything.

Having peace with God, access to God's grace and hope through the Holy Spirit, brings a sense of hope to our spirit that does not and will not disappoint us because it comes from God.

Two little boys were sitting at the lunch table at school. The first little boy looked in his lunch box and with a forlorn look on his face said, "My mom made me broccoli sandwiches for lunch today. Yesterday she made me liver sandwiches. The day before it was peanut butter and sardines. I think she's still getting even with me for that lamp I broke."

We can identify with that because, even though we know it's wrong, sometimes we try to get even. Sometimes we mistakenly think that's the way God acts, too. We want hope in our life. We want peace with God, but we're afraid God will just try to get even for all the stuff we've done that we know we shouldn't have done and for the things we have left undone that we know we should have done. But the Good News is that God is merciful and forgiving. All we need to do is repent and confess our sins. All we need to do is come to the one who can give us access to the grace of God, Jesus Christ, God's son. Through Christ's recommendation we discover we *can* have peace with God. And we discover God doesn't get even. God forgives. God seeks peace with us through Christ and the Holy Spirit.

Come to the Son. Pick up your recommendation. Experience firsthand, the hope that does not disappoint.

Corpus Christi

Our Daily Bread

1 Corinthians 11:23-26

After hearing in Sunday school about Jesus feeding the 5,000 from five loaves and two fish, a little boy was watching his mother make sandwiches and said, "Boy, Jesus sure must have sliced that bread awfully thin!"

Throughout time, grain and bread have been powerful symbols of life, vitality, sharing, nurture, the family, and even wealth. To produce or gather grain was the first requirement of life. To store it and hoard it was the first sign of wealth. To share it was the first sign of hospitality. We call it breaking bread together, even today.

Bread And Life

Bread embodies the very substance of life. We see it, touch it, smell it, and taste it every day. We take it for granted because we have it. We forget how important it is to our daily life until we don't have enough. And yet every time we pray the Lord's Prayer we pray for our daily bread. In our abundance we have it in many varieties. It comes in many shapes, colors, sizes, and flavors. There are certain things that wouldn't be right without a particular kind of bread being served with it.

Sausage gravy wouldn't be any good without biscuits to pour it over.

Chipped beef wouldn't be right without toast.

Neither would a bacon, lettuce, and tomato sandwich.

Bread is an important element of daily life. What's Italian food without a thick slab of garlic bread, bread so heavy in butter and garlic that you make sure your spouse has a piece, too? Otherwise you won't be able to kiss for a week.

And what's a big pot of beans or black-eyed peas without a hunk of hot cornbread?

What's a gyro without pita bread?

Or imagine a Big Mac without the sesame seed bun.

We eat all kinds of bread on a daily basis. We eat tortillas with Mexican food, crackers with chili, Texas toast with chicken fried steak, hot pastrami on rye, bagels with cream cheese or lox, toasted English muffins with jelly. Who could have a big family dinner without a basket of hot dinner rolls?

Bread is important. There's nothing in the world that excites the senses and brings back more memories than the smell of bread baking. It permeates every corner of the house. It lingers invitingly, tempting the taste buds. The anticipation tastes almost as good as that first thick slab, still steaming and hot from the oven, slathered with butter or honey and melting in your mouth.

Now that your mouth is watering thinking about bread and what you're going to have for lunch or why you didn't eat breakfast, think about this question. "Have you ever been really hungry? Have you ever gone without food for any significant length of time?"

There was a young man and his friend, both eighteen years old, who decided to hitchhike from Springfield, Missouri, to Washington, D.C., and then on up to New York City. They weren't the smartest of the bunch because they took off in November. It was cold and snowing. The further East they went, the colder it got and the more it snowed. They weren't having a whole lot of luck getting a ride — partly because of the weather and partly because of the way they looked. It was the 1960s. They both had long hair and bell-bottom jeans. Nobody was stopping.

It wasn't long before they ran out of money. They went for three days without food. Neither of them had ever been so hungry in all their lives. They eventually collected enough soda bottles to buy a loaf of day-old bread and a small jar of peanut butter. They were so hungry that turned out to be one of the finest meals either one of them had ever eaten.

Most of us never really experience that kind of hunger. All we ever have is that "stand in front of the fridge with the door open, I don't know what I want, but I want something 'cause I've got the munchies" kind of hunger. That describes our lives, too. There is a hunger like that munchie kind of hunger within us. We know we want something to satisfy that hunger, but we don't know what. And we don't know where to turn.

Bread is a powerful symbol in the Bible. All this talk about bread isn't meant to drive you crazy or make you so hungry you can't listen. But that hunger you're feeling right now can't begin to compare to the hunger the Israelites felt as they wandered in the wilderness after leaving Egypt. They hungered and prayed for bread to fill their aching, empty stomachs. And then there was Jesus' hunger. Imagine how hungry he must have been after spending forty days fasting in the wilderness. The temptation to turn stones to bread was very real.

There are other Biblical symbols of bread, as well. There is unleavened bread, prepared and eaten hurriedly on the night of the Passover, a night that families still celebrate today. There are the loaves and fishes that fed both 5,000 and 4,000. There is the bread of the last breakfast, the meal of bread and grilled fish Jesus served the disciples on the beach shortly before his Ascension. And there is the loaf of revelation at Emmaus, where Jesus revealed his risen self through the breaking of bread with two of the disciples who had given up hope.

The Last Supper

Who could forget the bread of the Last Supper where bread and wine on the table are transformed in significance, and Jesus becomes the loaf of life? Throughout his ministry Jesus said things like: "I am the bread of life ... I am the living bread that came down from heaven ... whoever feeds on this bread will never hunger and will live forever ... this bread I give for the life of the world."

At the Last Supper, Jesus broke bread with the disciples and prepared himself to be broken for our sakes. As we look at the elements — the common everyday types of bread — we are reminded of Christ's sacrifice for our lives, and it breaks our hearts to think that God loves us this much. We come broken by sin and broken by others. In that brokenness we come to the brokenness of Christ and we find wholeness.

In our hungering and thirsting we come to Christ who is hungering and thirsting for our salvation. In Christ we find satisfaction and fullness. In our brokenness, our hearts and spirits are healed and raised to new life in Christ. As we eat the bread of the Lord's Supper it ceases to be bread and becomes part of us. In the receiving we are consumed in the giving of ourselves to Christ. We rise in newness of life through him and in him. We look the same but somehow we are different. We are new from the inside out. We are fed and satisfied. We are clean and shiny. We glow from the grace of the one who invites us to this special table, our Lord and Savior.

And as we look out at those around us, we are reminded of the multiplicity of our responses and experiences. On every occasion that the Lord's Supper is celebrated we realize that as members of the church, we really are *one* Body, *one* Loaf in Christ, made of many grains. We are multinational, multiracial, multilingual, multicultural, and multigenerational. But we are made one in the Body of Christ. Out of our diversity comes unity through Christ. Today we affirm one Lord, one Savior, one Spirit, one Baptism, one God and Creator of us all. Today we affirm one loaf, the body of Christ.

Today we kneel before the Lord's table with men, women, and children around the world of every station and occupation. Today saints and sinners, royalty and commoners, priests and laity, righteous and unrighteous all kneel before Christ. The one thing that binds us together is that we all hunger and thirst and there is only one person who can satisfy that aching hunger. That person is Christ Jesus who gave his life for us.

When we eat the bread and wine, we remember Jesus' words found in Paul's letter: "This is my body that is for you. Do this in remembrance of me." In the same way he took the cup also, after supper, saying, "This cup is the new covenant in my blood. Do this, as often as you drink it, in remembrance of me."

We do this in remembrance and in amazement. Amazement because we marvel that the love of God could encompass and forgive the sins of the whole world. We marvel that the little morsel of everyday bread which we receive can satisfy a hunger such as ours. And yet it does, because it is a gift from God. It's just bread, but it's so much more. And it means so much more. It is the bread of life.

Come and join us in our celebration. Celebrate this simple yet elegant meal prepared just for you. Come. Be fed by the hand of the Savior, the Bread from Heaven. Don't go away hungry.

Proper 4 • Pentecost 2 • Ordinary Time 9

We Are Witnesses

Galatians 1:1-12

Have you ever been afraid? Of course you have; we all have. We've all had those times like the little boy who came running into the kitchen and asked his mother if he could watch a wildlife special on the educational channel. "Hurry, Mom, it's got lions and tigers and snakes and all kinds of wild animals. Please, Mom, can I watch it?"

Mom said, "Well, sure, you know it's all right to watch that station. And that sounds like a wonderful program for a brave little guy like you to watch."

The little boy looked up at his mother and asked, "Will you come watch it with me?"

"I'm sorry," Mom said, "but Mommy is kind of busy right now."

"But, Mom!" the little boy insisted, "You don't understand. You gotta watch it with me! I'm too scared to watch it by myself."

At other times we've been like the little boy who was in bed one night and hollered out to his mom. "I'm afraid of the dark!"

Mom tried to relieve his fears by saying, "There's no reason to be afraid of the dark. God made the dark as well as the light!"

The little boy thought about it a minute and then said, "Yeah, but God made alligators, too!"

Sometimes we're just afraid and want someone else's company throughout the adventure of life. Other times we're afraid and we don't really want our fears removed. We resist help from others or from God. We're like the second little boy, and we find lots of reasons not to trust God.

The Scripture tells us that the Galatians experienced fear also. They had heard the Good News of the resurrection. They had heard how the disciples had run out to the tomb and seen that it was empty. They had heard how two men had spoken with Jesus on the road to Emmaus. They had probably even heard that others had seen the risen Christ when he stood in their midst, not once but twice. Paul even told them his account of how he met the resurrected Jesus face-to-face on the road to Damascus while on his way to arrest these so-called Christians. And yet here they are turning away from the gospel which Paul shared with them. Maybe they were too afraid because of the pressures of society. Maybe there was one really strong, domineering individual who was leading them astray with this "gospel contrary to what we proclaimed." That might explain why Paul almost screams from the page, "Let that one be accursed!"

Something happened. They were slipping away, falling away from the gospel. They were thinking of all kinds of excuses not to trust God's promises.

But Paul knew God wasn't about to give up. He knew Jesus was alive. Paul knew that Jesus had defeated both sin and death. Jesus had wiped out the main source of all fear. So Paul wasn't about to let the Galatians or the mission of Christ and the Church become immobilized by fear or anything else. The stone had been rolled away; the tomb was empty. The Good News of forgiveness and grace had been given to Paul by Christ himself. Paul wasn't about to give up. He wanted the Galatians to be excited and empowered by this Good News and no other.

We Are Witnesses Of The Resurrection

Now granted, the gospel can be a little hard to understand. To the unknowing heart it has to sound as strange as something from the *X-Files* or the *Twilight Zone*. Someone being raised from the dead, making appearances, and popping up all over the place like some ghostly jack-in-the-box just doesn't make sense, without faith. Some ghost, who claims to be God, striking Paul blind because he was trying to arrest his followers, almost sounds like the plot to some kind of fantasy or science fiction novel.

The disciples used the Upper Room as their headquarters after the crucifixion and resurrection partly because it was safe. The news they had, the news they knew firsthand, was hard to believe. No wonder the Galatians, who had heard it secondhand from Paul, were having a hard time.

Why was it so hard for them to believe? Well, haven't you ever been told some piece of news that puzzled you or that just didn't sink in right away? Back in 1980, my wife Mary and I had been trying to have another child. We had one son but we wanted a larger family. I came home from seminary one Friday night ready to unwind and get ready for Sunday. I was sitting in my chair watching television. Mary came in, sat in my lap, and told me she thought she was pregnant. I don't remember what I said. I'm sure it was the appropriate thing, but to be really honest, it wasn't until Monday morning when I was headed back to seminary that it finally sunk in. The more it sank in, the more excited I became. But it took awhile for the news to penetrate this thick head of mine.

That's pretty much what happened to the Galatians and all the people of the early Church. It wasn't that they didn't believe; it's just that the news of the Resurrection was so good it was almost too good to be true. Consequently, it took awhile for it sink in. And even after it sank in it was still hard to believe. No wonder the Galatians were having a hard time.

Because of their confusion, it would have been easy for one of them who was a little more educated or appeared to be more educated slowly to lead them astray. It wouldn't have been anything big, just a little undermining of one portion. Make it sound reasonable and convincing and most people would begin to agree. Then challenge another aspect of the teaching in the same way. First there is just a tiny hole in the wall, but it grows bigger and bigger. And then they start working on the foundation. And slowly but surely, chip by little chip, the wall of faith begins to crumble.

No wonder Paul was so upset. He straightened things out in a hurry. He didn't want to have to keep re-teaching this group of people. Instead he wanted them to get on board and begin sharing the gospel. The real gospel, not some different gospel, but the gospel of salvation and eternal life through the death and resurrection of Jesus Christ the Son of God.

Paul and the disciples carried this message of repentance and forgiveness of sin to the far reaches of the world. They proclaimed the Good News and witnessed to the Resurrection. They had seen it change lives. They had witnessed the power of the message. The message didn't need to be changed. It didn't need to be diluted because it came directly from Christ.

Paul wanted the Galatians to be a part of this glorious ministry. He wanted them to put away their fears of not being accepted by the people around them. They weren't in the people-pleasing business but the world-saving business.

Paul spoke with such confidence and such challenge because he knew he had been a witness to something incredibly wonderful. He had been a witness to the resurrected Son of God, the Messiah for whom his people had waited centuries. And once he witnessed the Risen Christ, he knew that he couldn't do anything but share the Good News with others. And we are called to do the same. The Son of God calls us to be witnesses, and share the Good News, too.

And we *are* witnesses. When we look through the eyes of faith, we see evidence of the risen Christ every day. Every time we give ourselves in ministry, every time we extend a helping hand, every time a meal is shared with someone in need, whether at a night shelter, in a soup kitchen or within the membership of a church, we experience the resurrection. Every time the bell choir or the chime choir, the adult choir or the children's choir play or sing, we see signs of the resurrection. Every time someone makes an act of renewal or we baptize a baby, youth, or adult, we see signs of the resurrection. Every time a youth is brought closer to God and given the tools to walk through life unafraid, Christ is there. The Risen Christ is with us, that's why we do these things. Just like Paul, just like the disciples, just like the Galatians, we are witnesses.

We Are God's Children, Now

But we are more than witnesses, too. We have seen the risen Christ, but that's not the whole message. That's only part of the message. The rest of the message is that the risen Christ has come to take away and forgive our sins.

I remember a little boy in one church who told me one day that he wished he had a door in his heart. I asked him why. He said life would be so much easier if he could open up his heart and just get all the sin out.

I wish it were that simple. The message of Christ is clear. We are sinners. That's why he came. That's why he suffered and died on the cross. That's why he was buried and rose from the grave. Jesus came to redeem us and set us free. It's my understanding that the verb "to save" means "to be made whole." When we sin, we become broken. We break our relationship with God and with others. And we break ourselves.

Christ came to save us and make us whole again. Christ came to give us that second chance we all so desperately need, not because of anything we have done; not because we deserve a second chance, but simply because God loves us.

John's first letter tells us, "See what love the Father has given us, that we should be called children of God; and that is what we are."

We are called the "children of God." Not by the world, not by Christ, but by God. Through calling us children of God, God claims us and renews us and offers us new life. What better way to show us the depth and breadth and height of that love than to call us the children of God, to claim us as God's own?

There was a little boy who put a paper sack over his head and then prayed: "Lord, I'll tell you what I did today, but I won't tell you who I am."

At times we are just like that little boy. We would gladly confess what we have done, if we didn't have to let God know who it was. That embarrassment is really what drives us, finally, to repentance. It is the shame that we feel for our sinfulness, for the wounds we have caused God, for the broken relationship we have caused. And the Good News is that, "Beloved, we are God's children *now*." We don't have to wait for some far off, distant date. As God's children, *now*, we can claim our inheritance today. And our inheritance is forgiveness. God willingly forgives those who seek forgiveness and new life. God claims us as God's own, as one of God's children and takes the sack off our heads and our hearts.

And then, as children of God, we become living, breathing, visible, tangible, touchable witnesses of the resurrection. We are witnesses and we can humbly and joyfully say, "See what love God has given us, that we should be called children of God; and that is what we are."

Called To Invite Others To The Dance

As the children of God we have been called to be witnesses. Which means that we're called to a life of tangible evangelism. We're called to invite others to experience the love of God which we've experienced. We're called to share the Good News of God's love, the Good News of the Resurrection and the Good News of forgiveness and second chances with those around us. That is what drove Paul.

Remember the first dance you ever went to? A young man in the seventh grade thought it was going to be so much fun, he could hardly wait to get there. All of his friends were there. And so were the girls. That was the whole reason for going. They got to the school and they were so cool. But that dance turned out to be less than cool. You see, they wouldn't have needed any chaperones because nobody danced. Oh, a couple of the teachers got out there and tried to break the ice. And a couple of the girls danced with each other. But they didn't count. The boys and the girls lined up on either side of the gym and just stared at each other for the whole three hours of the dance.

The guys and the girls all went up and requested all the best records to be played. They enjoyed the music. This particular seventh grade boy and his buddies just stood around talking about how much fun it would be to dance and which of the girls they would like to dance with. They even got up the courage to talk to some of the girls. But none of them ever got around to asking anyone to dance.

They were all dressed up and ready to dance. They all had invitations to the dance. But none of the girls asked any of them to dance and they were too scared to ask any of the girls to dance with them.

Do you remember being invited to a high school party over at someone's house, only you weren't going with anyone at the time? You didn't have a steady girlfriend or boyfriend. You went and you felt out of place because everyone else had a date. So there you were, all by yourself with no one to ask you to dance.

As I think about it, those are both parables of the Church. You see, Jesus told the disciples, "You are witnesses." And he instructed them to go out and share with others their message, their Good News of redemption, forgiveness, and eternal life. We're called to do the same. We're called to share our message and invite others to the dance of faith. However, we're called to do more than just invite people to the dance. Lots of people come to the dance. They come to church week after week, but there is something missing. These folks are like that seventh grade dance and the high school party. They got an invitation to the dance but no one has asked them to dance.

In the Church, our business is to invite people to the dance. But it goes way beyond that too. We're called to teach those who don't know how to dance; how to dance the Lord's dance. And then we're called to invite them to dance. You see, a dance isn't a dance unless someone dances. And believe it or not, many folks want to be asked, not only to the dance, but they want to be asked to dance as well. They want to be a part of a community of faith. They want to be a part of something bigger than themselves. They want and need to be a part of a larger family which cares for and nurtures them.

About three days after that seventh grade dance, the boy who told this story found out that the one girl he had wanted to dance with the most would have danced with him. It turned out, that out of all the boys at the dance, she was hoping that he would dance with her. He really felt dumb, because all he had to do was ask.

For the most part, that's all we have to do. Sharing the witness of our faith, sharing the Good News of the resurrection, sharing the good news of forgiveness and redemption is simply inviting people to the dance. And when they get here, inviting them to dance. We are witnesses to the reality of the resurrection. We are witnesses to the power of redemption and forgiveness. We are witnesses to new life in Christ. We're called to invite others to experience the love of God and the dance of faith.

We have a wonderful message, full of hope and acceptance; a message full of the future. God loves us so much that God sent His only Son to give his life for us. God sent Jesus to show and tell the Good News, that we are part of the family of God, that we are the Children of God, *now*.

A young boy burst into the great throne chambers of a medieval king. The boy was skipping and singing as children do. He was completely oblivious to the regal sobriety of his surroundings.

Suddenly, he was intercepted by an armored guard. "Have you no respect?" hissed the soldier. "Don't you know that the man on the throne is your king?"

The boy wriggled out of the soldier's grasp. Then dancing away, he laughed and giggled and said, "He is *your* king but he is *my* father!" And the boy bounced up to the throne and leaped into the king's lap. And the king welcomed him with open arms and a smile on his face.

That's the kind of relationship God wants with each of us. There are people everywhere who have never heard this word of hope. They've never heard the Good News. They've never been asked to dance. They've never even gotten an invitation to the dance. Someone once wrote, "Hope is hearing the melody of the future. Faith is to dance to it." You and I are witnesses to the great Good News of Jesus Christ, the Lord of the Dance. We've heard the melody of the future. We know the hope Christ gives. We've taken that step of faith and begun to dance to the melody. We're called to invite others into this glorious relationship of love, acceptance, and forgiveness in Christ. We are witnesses of the resurrection. We are called to invite others to the dance of faith, and then ask them to dance.

As you go about your busy days this week, look around. Think about your coworkers, your friends, and your neighbors. Who can you invite to the dance? Look around the church. Who can you ask to dance?

We are witnesses. And just as the disciples discovered when Jesus appeared in their midst, there's nothing to fear because the

Risen Christ goes with you. Who can you invite to the dance? Who can you ask to dance?

And if you're here this morning and no one has ever invited you to the dance, then I invite you now. Join in this dance of faith. Give your life to Christ and know the love, acceptance, and forgiveness of God. There is nothing to be afraid of. The message hasn't changed even after all these years. We haven't added anything new and strange. The Risen Christ *is* with us. We are the children of God *now*. Let's dance.

Proper 5 • *Pentecost 3* • *Ordinary Time 10*

Born And Called

Galatians 1:11-24

In an old *Family Circus* cartoon by Bil Keane, the oldest little girl, Dolly, comes into the house all hot and sweaty and says, "Boy, it sure is human out there!"

We know what she meant. Even though she got the word wrong, she made a very profound statement. Sometimes we act so Christ-like. We do and say all the right things. As the Church, as the body of Christ and individual Christians, we claim to be on the narrow path, and sometimes it really does shine through. And then there are the other times when we're just so, well, human. Our humanity hangs out for all to see. Our fallen nature just pokes its ugly head through and reminds us just how much we have to depend on God's grace and how much we and the whole world still need the saving grace of Jesus Christ.

Dolly is right, not just about us but about the whole world. "It *is* human out there!" And that's both a blessing and a curse. It's both a joyous statement of our worth in the Creator's eyes; for as humans we were created in God's own image. And that's really something to be thankful and joyous about. "It *is* human out there!" But unfortunately that is also a head-hanging statement of shame for what we've done and how we've rejected God's will. It is a statement of shame on how we have wounded, broken, fractured, and nearly destroyed that image of God within us. We've so wounded and broken that image, that link between us and God, through our disobedience and sin, that we are estranged and alienated from God. "It *is* human out there!"

But the Good News is that through Christ, through his personal appearance and his obedient sacrifice on the cross for our sakes, we are no longer estranged and alienated. Through our acceptance of Christ we are forgiven, reconciled to, and brought back, *bought back*, into relationship with God. The image of God that was broken and wounded has been repaired, renewed, and healed through the power of Jesus the Christ, the Son of God.

That's our story. That's why we're here this morning. In some part, whether in fullness or not isn't important. But in some part we have been touched by and experienced that Good News. The death and resurrection of Jesus Christ for our sake has impacted our lives and we have become new creations in Christ. We are citizens of the Kingdom of God, people of the rolled stone and the empty tomb. We are the Resurrection people who have been raised to new life in Christ. And that is what brings us here. That is what empowers our lives, our work, our relationships with others. The seeds of faith have grown and blossomed and born fruit in our lives.

Back in the days when you rang the operator to put you through to the person with whom you wanted to talk, an elderly lady received a notice in the mail that she had won a sizable amount of money. She was so excited she rang up the operator and said, "Oh, just get me anybody!"

We know how she felt. God's grace, God's love has touched and renewed our lives. We have experienced the Good News, but there is more to do. It's not just enough to receive the Good News. So, what do we do? What do you normally do with Good News when you receive it? You pass it on, you tell someone else. That's our job.

We Are Sent

The Apostle Paul had been breathing murderous revenge upon the followers of this upstart Jesus. The disciples and the entourage which had witnessed the resurrection and whose lives had been changed, were bursting at the seams to tell someone, anyone, the Good News that Jesus was the long-awaited Messiah. They were bursting at the seams to tell anyone and everyone, so much so that they risked persecution. They were champing at the bit. Their engines were all revved up ready to go. They could hardly contain themselves.

And into this enthusiasm walked Paul. He couldn't believe it. These followers of Jesus were corrupting the faithfulness of his people. These followers of Jesus were leading people astray. They were giving them misinformation. That was dangerous to their spiritual health. Paul pleaded with the authorities to let him arrest these so-called Christians and put an end to this madness.

But little did Paul know of the power of Jesus. In a sense, Paul had become a religious bounty hunter. But he never got the chance to cash in his first bounty. God had other plans for Paul. On his way to make that first arrest, with warrants in his pocket, he was confronted on the road to Damascus by the Risen Jesus, the very one whose message he was trying to eradicate.

The irony of that encounter is that Paul had a life-changing moment. He was literally blinded by the Light of the world. And in a twist that only God could think of, Jesus called Paul into the same ministry as the disciples. God gave Paul the Holy Spirit and the authority needed for his office. And then God sent him out to carry the Good News of Jesus Christ and God's Kingdom. God sent Paul out to preach, to teach, to heal, and to confront evil wherever he found it, in the name of Jesus. Jesus sent him out to be a missionary to a world not so different than ours. It was "human out" back then, too. It was a world filled with the same sort of suffering and pain, the same sort of burdens that we face every single day. Paul was reborn that day and called to a different calling.

Oh, he had some preparation to do, but he would never be the same. And neither would the Church. He was born and called. He dropped his warrants and picked up his passport. He loaded his backpack and took off to spread the Good News throughout the known world. Just as his life was transformed, that warrant was transformed into ordination papers and a mission statement.

Just like Paul, just like the early disciples, we too are sent out with the Good News. We too are commissioned through our baptism and membership in the Church. We too are commissioned and given the authority to preach and teach, to heal and confront evil wherever it is found. We are born and called. We are sent to proclaim the faith and bring glory to God.

"It *is* human out there." We are all so bogged down with our own personal burdens that we can barely get out of our own way. We all drag so much baggage around with us that we can hardly even live. Often times we are so preoccupied with this baggage and these burdens that we can't focus on anything else. The truth is "it is *very* human out there" and we're called to help bear the burdens of others and to proclaim the Good News so that Christ can not only help bear but also lift the burdens from their hearts. We're sent as missionaries for Christ. We're sent to share the story and the glory of our faith in Christ with others.

In the sheep country of New Mexico, the shepherds were having trouble losing lambs in the late winter and early spring. It seems the ewes would take their lambs out to graze and late in the day it would start to snow. The temperature would drop and the ewes would continue to graze. Being tired, the lambs would lie down on the ground. But before long, because of the drop in temperature and the snow, the lambs would freeze to death. The shepherds got together to discuss the problem. The ewes, covered with thick wool didn't feel the temperature change. They didn't feel the cold. So, the shepherds came up with a unique solution. They took shears and sheared just the top of the head of the ewes. Then when the weather changed, they felt it and headed back to the barn, thus saving many of the lambs.

Sometimes our hearts get all warm and woolly. It's not wrong; we like that warm fuzzy feeling and we get comfortable with it. The trouble is, when we are so engulfed in that warm fuzzy feeling we can't feel the hurt and pain and discomfort others are feeling.

That's partly what was wrong with Paul. In a sense, it wasn't his heart so much as his eyes. In a sense, the wool had been pulled over his eyes and he couldn't see the truth. That was when God brought out the shears. The Holy Spirit needs to shear our hearts of some of that wool so we too can feel the hurt and pain and discomfort of those around us. When we share that pain and discomfort, then we can share the Good News and the healing power of Christ.

We are called to spread the Good News of the one who has lifted our burdens and set us free. We are called to spread the Good News of Christ who has sheared our hearts and lifted the wool from over our eyes. We are called to share the Good News of the one who will lift the burdens and baggage of life from the hearts of all who call upon him. What better message could we bear than one of forgiveness and new life?

We Don't Go Alone

It is exciting to think that you bear a message that can change the life and lift the burdens of those with whom you share it, isn't it? It is exciting and a little bit frightening, too. It is frightening to talk about something as personal as faith. It takes faith to talk about faith. And yet, we are sent to talk about faith, to preach Christ. And while that may be scary or frightening, we are not sent alone.

You did notice, didn't you, that Paul didn't go of his own volition. Paul was sent and he had a very special companion. No, it wasn't Silas or Barnabas. It wasn't Timothy or Titus. No, this companion is promised to each and every believer. This companion is the one promised by Jesus. The one who blew into the lives of the disciples and every believer on the day of Pentecost. This companion is the Holy Spirit. Jesus knew the kind of fear and anxiety that would come up when we mention the words evangelism or witnessing. Jesus did promise to be with us, even to the end of the age.

Jesus is with us, through the presence of the Holy Spirit. We never go alone because we go in the power of the Holy Spirit. That's awesome. It's mind boggling. Christ sends us out into the world to proclaim the Good News, equipped as he was equipped, with the presence and power of God's Holy Spirit. I personally can't think of any better companion, can you?

And not only is the Holy Spirit our companion, but through the Holy Spirit, Christ has already been where we are going. Jesus sent the seventy to where he intended to go. Jesus sent the twelve to where he intended to go. And Jesus sent Paul to where he intended to go.

Through God's prevenient grace, the Holy Spirit was and is already there whispering God's love song and preparing the hearts and souls of the people we will meet for the Good News which we carry. The Holy Spirit is already at work in the lives of any we might meet, any to whom we might have an opportunity to witness. God is already at work in their lives preparing the soil of their heart and soul for the planting of the seeds of new life which we bear in Christ's name.

A Gallup poll, taken in the spring of 1980, of people who don't belong to anyone's church, asked: "Would you join a church?" More than fifty percent indicated they would. And when they were asked why they hadn't joined a church, the response was, "No one has asked us."

That shows that God is already at work in their lives. Knowing that God has been there ahead of us and has been at work preparing their hearts for the message we bear takes much of the fear and anxiety away. Now all we have to do is like the Nike commercials say, "Just do it."

Just Do It

And you see, that's really all there is to it. We can give excuse after excuse, but in the end, that's all they really are — excuses. Jesus didn't say go and preach only if you're not scared. Jesus didn't say go and preach but only if you feel secure. That's not acting on faith. That's depending on safety. Jesus instructed Paul, who had been the chief enemy of the Church, to step out on faith and preach the Good News. Paul was called to trust in God's grace to see him through.

There was a young man who came to a pastor's office and said he wanted to be a Christian but he didn't know what being a Christian was all about. The pastor told the young man to read the Book of Acts as preparation, then come back and they would talk about what he had learned and how to apply it. A week went by and then another week and then another. The preacher began to think that he'd made a serious mistake in his suggestion.

Finally, almost a year later, the young man finally appeared. When the surprised pastor asked where he had been, the young man said, "You told me to read the book of Acts. Well, every time

I started to read it, it told me to go do something. So, I went and did it. I've just been too busy to get back."

That's the attitude we're supposed to have. We're sent to share the Good News of Jesus Christ and to invite others to join us on this journey of faith. We're sent to tell others about the one who will lift their burdens and give them new life. We're sent to live and act like our Lord and Savior Jesus Christ. That alone may very well be the most profound evangelism we can do. In many cases, the most effective message we can ever preach is the one we preach with our lives. We are sent by Christ.

The pundits say that e-mail has replaced the water cooler. People used to hang out at the water cooler and exchange news about the company or the people. They shared recipes and tips for getting along with the boss. In times of strife and change in the workplace people would often come to the water cooler and ask the same question. "What do you hear?" or "What have you heard?" They were looking for some news, good news, they hoped.

We have that Good News people are looking for. It's not our message but the message of the one who has saved us and sent us. It is the message of those who are born and called like Paul. "It's human out there!" This passage challenges us to be like Paul and to be about the business of sharing the Good News.

Who have you shared that message with recently? Are you living as one who is sent? Are you living so there's no doubt that you are one of the messengers? If not, then become one. Step out in faith. Let the wool of your heart be sheared so you can feel what others feel. Step out on faith and share the Good News. Join Paul and help others to glorify God because of you.

Proper 6 • *Pentecost 4* • *Ordinary Time 11*

By Faith In Christ

Galatians 2:15-21

There's a story about two newspaper editors who had been involved in a bitter feud of words and ideas for years. When one of the editors finally died, the other one took the opportunity to get in one last dig; he published the first editor's obituary under "Public Improvements."

Controversy has always been around, especially in religion and theology. Someone once said that if you put two theologians together in the same room and ask them a question, you wind up with three different opinions.

This passage from Galatians proves that controversy even touched the life of the early Church. It deals with one of the oldest controversies that the Church faced. This passage deals with the issue of law versus faith. The question was, "By which are we justified?" The answer Paul gives became a watershed decision which shaped the future of the Church.

The Law Versus Grace

What was going on here? Well, to boil it all down, Peter couldn't decide how he was supposed to live. When he was with the Jewish Christians, he followed all the Jewish laws and customs. But when he was with the Gentile (non-Jewish) Christians he didn't. That doesn't seem like too big of an issue at first, does it? Paul said we should be all things to all people. Peter did have that vision about reaching out to the Gentiles. And he did carry it out. But the issue grew because of the expectations of both groups. The Jewish

Christians expected all Christians to be like them and to follow all the Jewish customs and practices.

And their argument makes some sense. All the disciples were Jewish. Jesus was Jewish. They all followed Jewish customs and practices. Therefore, everyone else should, too. And that meant following the letter of the Jewish law.

But the Gentiles didn't know the customs and didn't understand the customs. Besides, they had accepted Christ, experienced the forgiveness of their sins, and been baptized without the law. Why should they turn around and suddenly have to have something new and strange thrust upon their relationship with God? It would sort of be like us saying to new members three months after they join, "Oh, by the way, we forgot to tell you, that after your first ninety days you have to shave your head and memorize a chapter of Revelation a week until you have the whole book memorized." Ridiculous, isn't it? (By the way — that letter goes out to new members next week.)

The real issue was, how do you become a Christian? Is it through following the law or is it through faith in Christ? The Jewish Christians were saying it was through following the law. And Peter was arguing on their side.

Paul was on the other side, arguing for faith and grace. Basically he says, "Look, I was a Pharisee all my life. No one knew the law better than I. I obeyed the law in all things. I was a Pharisee's Pharisee. But it didn't work."

"Instead of getting me closer to God, it only showed how much further away I had drifted. It wasn't until my encounter with Jesus on the road to Damascus that I understood the significance of faith and grace in my relationship with God."

Paul goes on to say, "No one will be justified by the works of the law." We are "justified by faith in Christ, and not by doing the works of the law." So, what does Paul mean?

When we try to experience salvation through "doing the works of the law," basically that means we've developed a checklist of sorts. This checklist is full of those things that we have to do or accomplish in order to be saved or to assure our place in salvation. Once we finish the list, then we're done; our place is assured. Right?

Unfortunately, with the law, it almost seems that for each item you check off the list, ten more appear. So, you find yourself running around in circles, out of breath, out of steam, never able to know whether or not you've made it or if you're even close to making it. Your faith becomes a chore not a joy.

Paul then goes on to say that if our salvation *is* based on a checklist of "doing the works of the law," then why did Jesus die on the cross? Either Jesus died so our sins can be forgiven and the relationship between us and God is healed *or* we can do the checklist thing and save ourselves through "doing the works of the law." But, we can't have it both ways. It really has to be one or the other. Is it the law or grace through faith in Christ? Is it the cross or the checklist? It can't be both. We know where Paul stood. He said, "If justification comes through the law, then Christ died for nothing."

So, how did this controversy turn out? Well, look at the altar. You don't see a checklist, do you? You see a cross.

Justification

We are justified by grace through faith in Christ. Let me repeat that. We are justified by grace through faith in Christ. Justification is a printers term and an old legal term. In printing you can see it today in word processing programs and in the newspaper. Notice the newspaper columns and how smooth the edges of each column are. The text has been justified. All the rough edges have been straightened out.

In old legal terms justification means to absolve or for the unrighteous to be made righteous by the judge.

Through our faith in Christ, the grace of God smoothes out our rough edges and evens up the ragged edges of our lives. Through our faith in Christ and the grace of God, God forgives us and absolves us of our sin and declares us righteous. It is not us who does this but God through Christ who does it for us.

Let's see if we can explain it this way. Imagine a family that likes dogs. In this family, both Mother and Father liked dogs. Mother always wanted a pretty little house dog. A "foo foo" dog as some people call them. Father always had hunting dogs. He loved to hunt rabbit and quail. At various times the family had beagles or bird dogs or both. Father believed that his dogs had to be purebred, and that meant they had to have papers. A dog just wasn't a good dog unless it had papers.

One summer morning the twelve-year-old son woke up and walked into the dining room. He saw bacon, scrambled eggs, and toast on the table, but there wasn't anyone around. He looked out the window into their backyard and, lo and behold, there, sleeping in one of the lawn chairs, was a puppy, about five or six months old. The boy grabbed a couple of pieces of bacon from the plate on the table and went outside. What the boy didn't know was that his grandmother, who was living with them at the time, had gone to get the father to chase this dog away.

When the boy approached the dog, it hardly moved at all. The dog's tail started wagging, but he just lay there, content in the lawn chair. When the boy presented the bacon, the dog finally lifted his head. The boy fed the dog the bacon, one small piece at a time. That was when it happened. The boy looked into the eyes of the puppy and the puppy looked into eyes of the boy and something clicked. The dog and boy were bonded for life. The boy named him Poochie.

The boy's parents weren't very thrilled about this bond at first. The boy didn't blame them. The dog had seen better days. Poochie was dirty. It looked like Poochie had been on the losing end of a fight. He had one chewed-up ear and a couple of cuts on his hindquarters. He had a piece of rope for a collar. And he didn't have papers. Mother and Grandmother both thought this dog was the ugliest thing they had ever seen. Grandma even tried to get the boy to name the dog "Ugly" instead of Poochie.

But to that boy, Poochie was the most wonderful dog in the world. He was the most beautiful dog he had ever seen, and despite the parents' best efforts, Poochie and the son became inseparable. They went everywhere together. Poochie's favorite game was fetch. Poochie loved to chase the ball and bring it back. He even became the center fielder when the children in the neighborhood played baseball. Poochie would bring the ball to whoever was at second base.

Poochie wasn't supposed to sleep in the house. He wasn't supposed to sleep on the boy's bed. But after awhile Poochie slept on the foot of the boy's bed every night. He became a part of the family and would curl up next to the boy whenever he laid on the floor watching television.

The only time Poochie's place was ever in jeopardy was when he ate the rocking chair that belonged to the boy's little brother. Poochie didn't really eat it, he just chewed up the end of one of the rockers while teething. Well, actually he chewed *off* the end of one of the rockers. Father had to replace it because the little brother kept falling over. Despite all that, Poochie was a part of the family.

Poochie's story isn't a faith story, but it illustrates what happens through our faith in Christ. You see, Poochie was nothing but a scraggly, old, lop-eared mongrel. He was a stray hound fit for the pound. He was worthless to Father because he didn't have papers. He wasn't purebred and he couldn't hunt. He was worthless to Mother and Grandmother because they thought he was so ugly. But in the eyes of that boy, he was the greatest dog that ever lived; a cross between Lassie, Rin Tin Tin, and Benjie.

And that's what counted. That's what was important and made all the difference to the parents. They judged Poochie harshly because he didn't meet all the criteria of their checklists. But that young boy looked at that dog through his heart. In a sense, that boy was Poochie's savior. It was his heart that bought Poochie's salvation. It was his heart that changed the parents' hearts and the way they looked at Poochie.

And that's exactly what Christ does for us. Looking through the eyes of the law, we can never measure up. We're just mongrels without papers or training. Looking through the eyes of the world we're ugly, scraggly, and lop-eared. Many of us don't measure up to even the lowest level of acceptability. We can't even begin to check off all the checks on those checklists.

But through our faith in Christ, God's heart is changed. God sees us through the eyes of the Son. God sees us and loves us because Christ loves us. We are "justified by faith in Christ." We are forgiven and made right with God and called righteous through that faith. That is both a very private and a very public improvement.

Our challenge is not to be consumed with the checklists of the law but rather to trust in Christ. Our challenge is to have faith in the one who changes God's heart. Look at the altar. There's no checklist there. But there *is* a cross. We are justified by grace through faith in Christ.

Proper 7 • *Pentecost 5* • *Ordinary Time 12*

Heirs According To The Promise

Galatians 3:23-29

As the lights in the movie theater dimmed, a young man loaded down with popcorn, cokes, and candy paced up and down the aisle, scanning the darkened rows. It was obvious he was looking for the person or persons with whom he had come. After three or four unsuccessful trips, he finally stopped and asked loudly, "Does anybody here recognize me?"

We all want to be recognized, don't we? We all want to belong. We all want to be known by others and to know that someone out there knows who we are and cares about us. We have a need to belong, to be in community together. That's why we join clubs, fraternities, sororities, civic organizations, sports teams, PTA, and even churches. We have a need to be in community with others just like us or close to being like us. That's part of how we are wired.

Belonging

Belonging is important because it's the way God created us. We are meant to be in community with one another. God created Adam and Eve together so they wouldn't be alone; so they would have support, nurture, and care. Even Jesus needed that support. The first thing he did when he began his ministry was to gather a small circle of friends. A group who would eventually become the leaders of the early Church. Yes, he needed to train them but Jesus also needed their support and their friendship. He even sought their counsel from time to time. At Caesarea Philippi, Jesus asked them who the crowds said he was. To show how important that relationship was to Jesus, at the Last Supper, he told them all. "I no longer call you servants ... now I call you friends" (John 15:15).

The disciples needed that assurance and that sense of belonging, too. In telling them that he was going away, Jesus reassured them that they would not be alone. Jesus said, "I will not leave you orphaned; I am coming to you" (John 14:18).

Belonging is important because it gives us a sense of self-worth and strengthens our own personal self-image.

A man I know grew up with two names. His mother divorced his father when he was nine months old. His real father chose to have nothing to do with him, so he didn't feel like he belonged to his father. His mother remarried and for the next fifteen years he went by his stepfather's name, not his father's name. He knew what his real name was. That was the name that appeared on his birth certificate and later on his driver's license, but he went by his stepfather's last name because that's what his mom and stepdad wanted.

But his stepfather never legally adopted him. The man never really figured out why. He thinks it was because they couldn't afford it. Consequently, he never really felt like he belonged to his stepfather, either. He didn't feel like he belonged to anyone. He had two names. He was both but neither. It wasn't until he enlisted in the military that he started using his real, legal last name. On that first day of boot camp they started calling roll and called out this young man's last name and no one answered. He wondered who that dim bulb was who didn't know his own name. Then he realized that he was that dim bulb. He suddenly took on a new identity. However, he was still both but neither.

He struggled with that dual identity until his mid-thirties. That was when he realized that neither of those names really mattered. By giving his life to Christ, his identity had totally and completely changed. It was no longer necessary to be either. It didn't matter which name he used because he was a new creation. He didn't need to feel rejected by a father who never wanted anything to do with him or a stepfather who didn't adopt him, for whatever reason.

The thing that made this happen were these words from Paul. They grabbed his attention. They jumped off the page and into his heart and soul and gave him new life. Suddenly it sank in. He was and is loved by our Heavenly Father. He was a child of God, a part of the family, and a part of the inheritance. Do you know how much power that promise has in it? Do you realize or know how freeing that is?

It's important that we know we have value. It's important that we know we belong.

We Are Heirs

This passage from Paul's letter to the Galatians shows us the value we have in God's eyes. Through our faith in Christ, we not only have value, but we are made heirs with Christ. "Heirs according to the promise." That is such a wonderful phrase. "Heirs according to the promise." Those are such powerful words; words of belonging and acceptance. Words of value.

Through our faith in Christ, we are made heirs with Christ. Heirs, not second class citizens. Heirs, not the ugly, unwanted stepchildren who begrudgingly have to be cared and provided for. Heirs, not orphans who are either left to fend for themselves or are thrown the scraps and leftovers, but heirs, joint heirs with Christ.

A Sunday school superintendent was registering the children in Sunday school and she asked two brothers their ages and birthdays. The bolder of the two boys said, "We're both seven. My birthday is April eighth and my brother's is April twentieth."

The superintendent was a little confused and said, "But that's impossible!"

The quiet brother answered, "No, it's not. One of us is adopted."

Before she was even aware that she had asked, the words were out, "Which one?"

The boys looked at each other and smiled. Then the bolder one said, "We asked Dad that question once, but he just said he loved us both so much that he couldn't remember any more which one was adopted."

Through our faith in Christ we are made heirs with Christ. That means that we have equal access to God. We are seen as equal heirs with Christ. There is no longer any distinction between us and Christ. We are brothers and sisters with Christ Jesus. God just loves us and can't remember any more which ones of us are adopted.

That's what faith in Christ does for us. We can hold our head high because we belong. We belong to God's family. We know our value, we know our worth, not by worldly standards but by God's standards.

The Promise

We are created in God's image, and through our faith in Christ we are made heirs of God's Kingdom, heirs according to the promise. And what is that promise? Well, it's actually more than one. It is all the promises of the Bible. We are heirs of all the promises God made with God's people. Promises like:

Exodus 6:7: "I will take you as my people, and I will be your God."

Joshua 1:5: "I will never leave you nor forsake you."

Matthew 28:20: "Remember, I am with you always, even to the end of the age."

Matthew 7:7: "Ask, and it will be given you; search, and you will find; knock, and the door will be opened for you."

Matthew 11:28: "Come to me, all you that are weary and are carrying heavy burdens, and I will give you rest."

John 14:18: "I will not leave you orphaned."

John 3:36: "Whoever believes in the Son has eternal life."

There are hundreds of other promises as well. There are promises that we can and should claim. There are promises that are ours because we are heirs with Christ and they are part of our inheritance.

We are reminded of these promises through the power of God's Holy Spirit. Like a parent holding and rocking one's baby, whispering all of the dreams and possibilities for that baby's future, the Holy Spirit whispers God's love song of faith in our ear. Like a parent encouraging one's child through some time of crisis or cheering them on in some time of joy, the Holy Spirit speaks those same words of encouragement to us.

Sometimes we listen and grow in the faith. Sometimes, just like our children listening to us, we ignore them or get distracted by the glitter of the world. But always God continues to tell us we are heirs with Christ. Heirs according to the promise. We may fail but God never does.

There may be times when we forget the promises or fail to listen to the promptings of God's Holy Spirit. There may be times in our lives when we get lost in the darkness of the world and cry out like the man in the theater: "Does anybody here recognize me?" That's when a hand goes up and God says, "Yes! You belong to me."

So remember: You have value. You are of infinite worth to God who created you in God's own image. And if that's not enough, then remember this: God sent Jesus just for you. Through your faith in Christ, you are an "heir according to the promise," a joint heir with Christ. That is the Good News. What better news could there be? Make it your own.

Proper 8 • Pentecost 6 • Ordinary Time 13

Life In The Spirit

Galatians 5:1, 13-25

According to one legend, at the signing of the first draft of the Declaration of Independence, John Hancock, one of the signers, the one with the biggest signature, is supposed to have said: "Gentlemen, we must be unanimous; we must all hang together."

After hearing this, Benjamin Franklin supposedly replied, "We must indeed all hang together — or, most assuredly, we shall all hang separately."

Whether or not that particular story is true, it still gives us insight into the minds and hearts of the founders of our country. It shows the great personal loss they and their families faced in committing themselves to the Declaration of Independence.

Independence Day is the day we in America celebrate the signing of that great article that set into motion the founding of this great country of ours — a country based on freedom.

Freedom

Freedom is one of those words that we use almost without thinking. Although it is a small word, only containing seven letters, it is huge in its concept and meaning. It is more than just a word. It is a whole philosophy and way of life and a thought process that is all summed up in seven letters. Freedom is not just a word; it is a noble word. It is one of those words and concepts that is worth dying for. Unfortunately though, we all seem to have our own concept of what freedom is and isn't. Or maybe it would be more fair to say that we have our own interpretation of the word and concept.

For some, especially for those who seem to have enough of anything and everything that money can buy and a desire to protect it, freedom means: "Leave us alone."

For those who don't have enough and desire the opportunity to better themselves; freedom takes on new meaning. It means: "Give us a chance."

Then there are those who don't have enough and don't want the opportunity to better themselves; they just want anything and everything that money can buy. For them freedom means, "Give me what you've got." Freedom can be interpreted to mean all kinds of things.

Faith

Here in Galatians, Paul begins by talking about freedom. But as you read this passage you see that Paul is saying that true freedom comes from faith in Christ. Paul asserts that apart from Christ, we cannot really know true freedom. Paradoxically, freedom comes through giving oneself to Christ. Once we give ourselves to Christ, then we are called upon and empowered to live the Christian life. Here, Paul reminds us of both the Christian life, a "life in the Spirit," and its alternative, "life in the flesh."

He cautions us and says, "For freedom Christ has set us free" (5:1). And then he reminds us not to let our freedom become "an opportunity for self-indulgence" (5:13) by giving us this long list of attitudes and actions to avoid.

During an elementary camp one summer, one of the volunteers was leading a discussion on the purpose God had for everything God created. They began to find good reasons for clouds and trees and rocks and rivers and animals and just about everything else in nature. Finally, one of the children asked, "If God had a good reason for everything, then why did God create poison ivy?" The discussion leader sort of gulped and, as she struggled with a way to answer the question, one of the other children came to her rescue and said: "The reason God made poison ivy is because God wanted us to know there are certain things we should keep our cotton-pickin' hands off."

I think that's pretty much the reason for this list of the works of the flesh. Paul wants us "to know there are certain things we should keep our cotton-pickin' hands off."

Fruit

While the passage includes the things we should avoid, it is more concerned about faith and about "life in the Spirit." If we accept that "freedom comes from faith in Christ" then we must also accept that our faith does more than just bring freedom. Part of freedom and part of faith is bearing fruit.

Paul gives a list of the spiritual fruit we should bear. He says, "The fruit of the Spirit is love, joy, peace, patience, kindness, generosity, faithfulness, gentleness, and self-control." Paul reminds us that this is not a list of fruit that we have to try to produce all by ourselves. Through our faith in Christ and living for Christ, we can have the guidance and the power of God's Holy Spirit to help us bear the fruit of the Spirit.

A couple of years ago some friends were in Mesa Verde, Colorado, on vacation, looking at the Pueblo Cliff Dwellings. In several spots you can look down into the valley. At one stop there was a drop of a couple of thousand feet. While looking down at that panoramic view, they noticed something near the valley floor. The telephoto lens showed there were a number of hawks or eagles flying with gentle flapping motions. All of a sudden there was a change. Catching one of the warm air currents rising off the valley floor, they stopped flapping their wings, and within just a minute or two these friends watched the eagles rise to where they were at least a hundred feet over their heads.

Those hawks or eagles could have flapped and flapped their way to that height, but they didn't need to, for they had caught a thermal! For me that is a great visual image of Isaiah 40:31, "God will raise you up on eagle's wings." And it's a great image of life in the Spirit. In a sense, those eagles or hawks trusted in God, for they trusted in what God had created and they were lifted up.

Sometimes we struggle with our faith. Sometimes we put out so much effort into trying to do the work of God that we never trust what God has created. One of the characteristics of a life in the

Spirit is trusting in God's Holy Spirit as your guide. When we trust in the Spirit we can begin to bear the fruit of the Spirit.

Paul names the fruit of the Spirit. And just like any fruit, the best way to describe it, is to let you taste it. And the best way to let you taste the fruit of the Spirit is through a couple of stories.

Five-year-old Kyle showed his church what Christian action is all about during their annual Easter egg hunt. Andrew is only two but he wanted to be out there with all the other preschool children hunting for eggs. Andrew found one right off, but his little legs were so short that he couldn't keep up with the other preschoolers. Kyle noticed that Andrew wasn't finding any eggs and he began an act of selfless, Christ-like love. Kyle started running just a little ahead of Andrew and putting the eggs he had found down for Andrew to find. Children don't always get it right, but sometimes they are God's messengers sent so that we can hear the Word of God and see the risen Christ in fresh ways.

Andrew's eyes glowed with joy. And Kyle was an example of "love, joy, generosity and gentleness." Kyle lived a life in the spirit. A life that in one simple act bore much fruit.

Let me share one more. There was a young couple in a particular congregation who had three children, the youngest of whom was a three-year-old girl. At a family gathering this little girl wanted to say the blessing before the meal. Everyone bowed their heads and the little girl prayed. When she finished her prayer she turned to her mother and asked, "Do you think God liked that prayer, Mama?"

Mom, of course, said, "Yes!"

That prayer was probably received with hugs and kisses and a ton of delight from God. How could God not receive such an innocent and heartfelt prayer from anyone?

Paul tells us "the fruit of the Spirit is love, joy, peace, patience, kindness, generosity, faithfulness, gentleness, and self-control." Despite her young age, that little girl lives a life in the spirit and bears much fruit.

And that's what we are called to do. We're called to live a life in the Spirit. You don't have to be a rocket scientist. You don't have to be perfect. You don't even have to be the best. You just have to have faith in Christ. You have to trust the guidance of God's Holy Spirit. And you have to spread your wings. But the Good News is that God will lift you up. And like those mentioned, you will bear much fruit.

In an old *Dennis the Menace* comic strip by Hank Ketchum that appeared on December 8, 1992, good old Mr. Wilson and his wife are standing at the front door. In the distance Dennis the Menace is waving good-bye. Mrs. Wilson says, "Alice says he was such a good baby." Mr. Wilson comments, "Obviously he got over it."

While that's very true of Dennis the Menace, it is also very true of each of us. We are born in the image of God, but somewhere along the line we experience our own fall. And we're never quite as good as God intended. But our faith in Christ changes all that. Christ gives us new life and freedom from the old life. Christ empowers us to be all that God created us to be. The Holy Spirit empowers us to bear much fruit as we live the freedom Christ has given us. "For freedom Christ has set us free," freedom to live a life in the Spirit. Accept that freedom and spread your wings.

Proper 9 • *Pentecost 7* • *Ordinary Time 14*

Bear One Another's Burdens

Galatians 6:(1-6) 7-16

The composer Bizet was the original bad luck man. He stayed up nights to finish an opera by the deadline, only to find out afterwards that the production had been postponed for a year. He wrote a symphony and misplaced the manuscript before anybody could play it. He entered a composing contest with only one other entrant, and ended up with second prize. Once he went to visit his girlfriend and tapped on her window at the very moment her mother was emptying a chamberpot from the room directly above his head.

Have you ever noticed that some people always seem to be in the wrong place at the wrong time? Do you ever get the feeling that life is not fair? That's a universal feeling. It was an issue that Jesus addressed in the Sermon on the Mount when he said, "God makes the sun rise on the evil and on the good, and sends rain on the righteous and on the unrighteous" (Matthew 5:45).

This feeling of unfairness within each of us is a sign pointing to God. We want to see justice done. We want to see wrong righted. We want to see the good guy win. And we feel cheated if virtue does not triumph. Feelings like that are so universal that C. S. Lewis believed they are evidence that we are created in the image of God. And believing that helps us in times of struggle and times of tragedy.

A close friend's parents were murdered and the tragedy really hit their pastor hard. Maybe it was because of the friendship. Maybe it's because he knew the love the surviving son has for God and the joy he always gets out of sharing that love in quiet yet powerful ways. Maybe it was because of the son's involvement in prison ministry that makes this seem so ironic. He struggled partly because the daughter-in-law is a Methodist minister and a part of him wanted to say this shouldn't happen to ministers. Aren't they somehow exempt from this kind of thing? Isn't there some clause in the ordination service that says clergy suffer *with* their congregations and that makes them exempt from suffering in general. And then reality set in. No one is exempt from tragedy. Not only *can* this happen to a minister's family; tragedy happens in *all* families. There is nothing that makes any one of us exempt from suffering and tragedy.

So, why does it happen? Where do we turn? What keeps us going when tragedy strikes?

The World Is Unjust

The why is simple. We don't live in a perfect world. In a perfect world, courts act swiftly and with justice. Our world is imperfect. And we're imperfect; we're lost.

A pastor was walking around the church early one Sunday morning and saw a sight that struck a chord in his heart. Sitting on the table near the sanctuary entrance was the Lost and Found box. Nothing spectacular, just a cardboard box with the words Lost and Found written in magic marker on the side. But in the box, nearly filling it, was some little girl's doll. The way the doll was laid in the box is what struck him. The doll looked as if she was resting comfortably in the box waiting for her little girl to come claim her. Her arms were extended out and it looked as if she were saying, "Please come get me. I'm lost and I need to be found. Please hunt for me and take me home."

He probably would have forgotten all about that doll if he hadn't been there to witness the reunion between that doll and her little girl. The little girl saw her doll, rushed over, grabbed her up, hugged her really tight and said, "There you are. I've looked all over the place for you. I missed you so much." And then, still hugging the doll, she went about her business as if the doll had never been gone.

And that is so very much like us, isn't it? Sometimes we think that God has forgotten us or left us lying on the pew in church, when in reality, it is we who have lost our way. Like that doll, we are lost.

God wouldn't need to look for the lost if we weren't lost. And God wouldn't have needed to send Jesus if we weren't lost. How could someone do what was done in the Columbine High School if they weren't lost? How could someone have murdered this pastor friend's parents if they weren't lost?

You see, apart from God we don't have a clue how to live or act. And we don't have a clue of how to get back into relationship with God. And it is because of that lostness that incomprehensible tragedies happen. Tragedies are *not* God's will. They are caused by someone else's will getting in the way of and superseding God's will. God's will is life and a loving relationship with each of us, not death and destruction.

We may live in a world that is lost, but the Good News is that Christ searches for us. We don't have to go in search of our salvation; God came to us in Christ, the Good Shepherd. God loves us so much that Christ sought us out. And if we will but stretch out our arms to God through Christ, then we will become the Lost who have been Found.

Turn To God

But where do we turn when tragedies in life do happen? We turn to God in prayer, just as Jesus said. And we turn to each other. Paul tells us to "bear one another's burden." And he says, "Let us not grow weary in doing what is right, for we will reap at harvest time, if we do not give up. So then, whenever we have an opportunity, let us work for the good of all, and especially for those of the family of faith."

The resources to get through tragic events don't come from us. They come from outside. They come from Christ's presence through the Holy Spirit in our lives. How do we get through together? Like the Church has always gotten through, we hold each other up. We depend upon the grace of God. We "bear one another's burdens."

Part of what gets us through these times is simply the Church: the work, the people, and the ongoing ministry of the church. That is driven home every Sunday morning. Despite the horror and tragedy of events — the message is still proclaimed; God's work is still done. Each Sunday men and women give testimony to their faith through great messages and sermons. Every Sunday people stand up and witness to their faith through testimony, praise, and song. The message of hope lives on as a family brings their children to be baptized.

When that happens the members of the church take vows to live their lives before the children so the children might see Christ living in the members. Members take vows to live their lives before the children so the children might be encouraged and grow to be like Christ by following the members' example.

Those are all part of the ministry of hope which we proclaim. During tragedies, it is a struggle to remember that hope. Sometimes it takes awhile. Do you want to know what really brought it all home for that pastor? The Sunday after the murder, his church had a potluck dinner and fundraiser for the youth. As this pastor stood in the dinner line, his friend called and said the family wanted him to preach the funeral. To be honest, he didn't want to do it, but he couldn't and wouldn't and didn't say, "No."

He cried and prayed with that pastor. But then had to go back into the fellowship hall and get himself back together. He cried a little and prayed a lot, then went back to the dinner. During that dinner he had a sacramental moment with an eight-year-old boy. The pastor had a bowl with potato chips in it and the boy wanted to know what kind they were. So the pastor told him, "They're mesquite barbecue."

The boy said, "Oh, I like those ... I think." So, the pastor moved the bowl over and asked if he'd like to try one. The boy tried one and he did like them, so they shared that bowl of mesquite barbecue potato chips together. They talked about all those little boy things while they ate. And when the bowl was empty, the boy jumped down. The pastor thought he was going off to play, but instead he brought back another bowl and said, "Preacher, now you have to share mine." And they did.

That sharing is a perfect example of the work of the church. As the Body of Christ we are called to share one another's joys and especially one another's burdens. We do it across meals, before and after meetings, during worship and Sunday school, in the grocery store, at fall festivals, and in the midst of tragedy. Our spirits groan in agony and concern for those who suffer, for those who lose loved ones. We empathize because we care. It hurts us because part of the body of Christ, our brothers and sisters in Christ, hurt. We hurt with them but we also find healing in that sharing.

Another place to which we turn is the Bible. We search the Scripture for the promises of God and claim them for our own.

What are those promises? Jesus said, "I will not leave you orphaned." "If I live you also shall live." And how about: "Will not God grant justice to his chosen ones who cry to him day and night? Will he delay long in helping them? I tell you, he will quickly grant justice to them."

And at the close of the Last Supper, just before Jesus prayed for the disciples and the Church, he said, "I have said this to you, so that in me you may have peace. In the world you will have trouble. But take courage; I have conquered the world!" (John 16:33). The list could go on and on because the Bible holds promise after promise of comfort and strength in times of trouble. We're called to claim them.

Never Give Up

Have you seen the poster which shows a crane or a heron standing in a marsh? The crane has a frog half way in its mouth and the crane's eyes are bulging. The reason for the crane's bulging eyes is that the frog isn't going easily, it has its front legs wrapped tightly around the throat of the crane. The caption of the poster says, "Never give up!" That's the kind of faith we should have. Because of the promises of God, we're called not to give up.

Recently I read the story of a boy who was dying of muscular dystrophy. After making his peace with his family and friends, he asked his father to arrange his body in such a way that he would die "in an impudent position." I like that story. I think it shows great faith. I'm positive that this young man will meet God and continue an ongoing conversation about fairness and justice. There's one thing for certain; with that attitude, he never gave up.

Tragedy can do one of two things. It can take the wind out of our sails and cause us just to give up. It can cause us to close and lock our doors and windows. It can cause us to build higher privacy fences and install stronger locks. It can cause us to barricade ourselves in fortresses. Or it can fuel the fire of our passion for spreading the Good News of salvation and bringing people to Christ, because Christ is the only one who can save the lost and bring them home. The one way protects us for a little while. The other brings light in the place of darkness and changes lives.

We're called never to give up and to continue to do the work of the Church. We're called to proclaim the faith, to proclaim resurrection in the face of death, to proclaim forgiveness and reconciliation. We're called to bear one another's burdens.

So, keep bearing one another's burdens and pray. Sometimes it may seem like there is never going to be an answer, but God does answer our prayers. God listens to our petitions and answers. You may not think prayer makes much of a difference in anyone's life, but I can tell you that prayer changes people; prayer changes lives. Prayer is heard and answered.

Let me tell you a story of answered prayer. One Sunday night one of our member's granddaughter got into a bottle of Tylenol and overdosed. They rushed her to the hospital, but her chances didn't look good. She couldn't keep down the medicine that was vital to her recovery. The doctors and pharmacists researched other ways to administer it but the only safe way was orally. On the last attempt, that now or never moment, she kept the medicine down.

There was a sigh of relief. But the doctors told them she wasn't out of the woods. Her liver wasn't functioning correctly. They could expect she would need to undergo a liver transplant. That was the news the church got on Monday morning. The family had already called several prayer groups and gotten their granddaughter on their lists.

Wednesday afternoon, to the doctors' and nurses' surprise, the granddaughter went home. All the tests showed that everything was normal. She was up playing like nothing had happened. The doctor said it was a miracle. Prayer did that. Bearing one another's burdens did that.

Do not lose heart. "Let us not grow weary in doing what is right, for we will reap at harvest time, if we do not give up. So then, whenever we have an opportunity, let us work for the good of all, and especially for those of the family of faith."

Proper 10 • *Pentecost 8* • *Ordinary Time 15*

Get Your Transfer Here

Colossians 1:1-14

Growing up, many kids love baseball. They love everything about it. They love playing it. The neighborhood kids divide up the big kids and little kids, so the teams are even, and then play inning after inning of baseball or softball either in a front yard or a back yard.

Kids of all ages love collecting baseball cards. Many of the kids my age loved to listen to baseball on the radio. I remember afternoon games, with the radio turned up really loud. The kids would play while they listened. Sometimes they would play flip cards while listening. It's obvious, by the excitement it generates, that baseball is still much loved.

The best thing about baseball was, and is, going to a game. There is something about being in the park. Maybe it's the hot dogs and big pretzels. Maybe it's the slim possibility of catching a foul ball or a homerun ball. I really think it's just the thrill of the game.

Thirty-five years ago, a certain young man started going to baseball games when he was about twelve or thirteen. His father's supervisor lived down the street. The company his father worked for had season tickets. One time the supervisor dropped by and, right in front of the boy, offered those tickets to the boy's father.

Now the boy's father wasn't much of a baseball fan. He certainly wasn't one who enjoyed going to the game. But the father did something that day that the boy would never forget. When offered the tickets, the father looked at his son and said, "Sure, I can use them." Then, when the supervisor left, that father gave those tickets to see the St. Louis Cardinals to his son and three of his son's friends.

The boys all thought the father was going to take them to the ball park. Instead, they went on an adventure. You see, St. Louis has a great public transportation system. Buses run everywhere. There was a city bus stop about a mile from their house. None of the boys had ever ridden anything but the school bus, but their parents had grown up riding the bus. Consequently they didn't think anything about letting the boys ride the bus into downtown St. Louis and the ball park. Of course, 35 years ago, the streets seemed a lot safer.

Anyway, the father took the boys down to the bus stop. He waited with them until the right bus came along and put them on the bus. He told them how to buy a transfer from the driver. And he even talked to the driver. It cost them a whole 65 cents to ride the bus. That first ride was kind of scary though, because they really weren't too sure about that transfer stuff.

When it was time to get off at the transfer stop, the bus driver took time to help them and remind them which bus they needed to get on. The bus driver even made them buy a return ticket and transfer so they wouldn't spend all their money on popcorn and cokes and not be able to get back home. And then he warned them: "Remember now, get on bus number so and so. Don't you be getting on any other bus now, or you'll get lost."

And then the bus left. The boys watched half a dozen buses pull up but they were the wrong ones. They even argued over whether to get on one bus or not because it said it was going to the ball park. But instead, they waited and got on the bus that driver told them to get on.

They made it to and from the ball game just fine. The transfer went without a hitch. As a matter of fact, that was the start of something great. Whenever the father's supervisor had tickets (they were about halfway down the first base line, five rows back) the boys got them. For three dollars they could ride the bus to the ball game and have a coke, popcorn and either a hot dog or a pretzel. Those were the days.

They had a great time. One of the things the young man really remembers, though, is that first trip on the bus. He remembers how scared he was about getting on the wrong bus, though, of course, he didn't want to tell his father or his friends. And then how safe he felt in the hands of that kind bus driver. And how excited he felt when they made that transfer and got on the right bus to the ball park.

So how does all of that fit with today's passage? In his letter to the Colossians, Paul talks about how "God has rescued us from the power of darkness and transferred us into the kingdom of God's beloved Son."

The young man and his friends put their trust in that kindly bus driver. As a result, they successfully transferred to the right bus and made their final destination, the ball game. Paul says that through our faith in Christ, through our redemption and forgiveness, our transfer has already been purchased and made. We've been given proper directions. And in essence, he echoes the bus driver: "Remember now, don't you be getting on any other bus, or you'll get lost."

Paul then goes on to list some prayer concerns he has for the Colossian Church; some concerns that will make them stronger Christians now that they have been transferred into God's kingdom. He prays that they might be made strong through the power of God, that they might have patience and endurance and that they might joyfully give thanks to God in all things. Those are the very things we're going to look at.

Strength

The first thing Paul asks for is that they be strong. But notice this isn't physical strength. This isn't strength that comes from them or from their inner fortitude and resources. This isn't the sort of strength we see in the heroes of the action adventure movies. You know the ones who take on the forces of evil and in a major fight scene are shot, stabbed, and pummeled to the point they can't stand. Then all of a sudden they draw on some inner resource that allows them to have almost super-human strength and abilities. With one mighty act of will and strength they vanquish the villain. That's not the kind of strength Paul is talking about. This strength has its origins in God's grace. Paul prays: "May you be made strong with all the strength that comes from God's glorious power" (1:11).

Paul is reminding them and us that try as hard as we might, none of us can do it on our own. In the world we may be expected to, but in the Kingdom of God, we're called to trust God and rely upon God for strength.

There is a brief story that illustrates this quite well. It seems there was a little boy who was helping his dad work in the garden. One of the things they were doing was picking up rocks. Everything went along fine until the boy came to a fairly large rock embedded firmly in the ground. Dad watched as the boy pushed, pulled, and did everything in his power to move that rock. But it didn't budge. The more he tried, the more frustrated he became. The father walked over and asked his son, "Are you using all of your strength?"

The boy said he was, and the father replied, "No, you're not ..."

The boy stopped and looked at his father, giving him one of those, "What are you, some kind of idiot?" looks that kids can give.

And then the father finished by saying, "You haven't asked me to help."

There is so much power for living the faith that is available from God. All we have to do is get on or stay on the right bus, the bus of grace, not works. We've been transferred into the Kingdom, all we have to do is call upon and rely upon the "strength that comes from the glorious power of God."

We can do that; we can stay plugged in to God's power through daily prayer — that personal time with God. We can stay plugged in through devotional time. It focuses our hearts and minds on God. We can stay plugged in through daily and ongoing Bible studies. They keep us in touch with God and strengthen us with the "strength that comes from God's glorious power."

Patience

Second, Paul prays that they have endurance and patience. I have always been in awe of long distance runners; those folks who have the stamina to run in a marathon. I know a young man, who, when he was in the ninth grade, decided to try out for the track team. It was there that he first saw the training that cross country runners went through. He was a sprinter. He didn't have the stamina for the long distance. He could run fast for short periods of time, but he didn't have the training or the endurance for the long distances.

I think a lot of people today are living life and faith like sprinters. We have heard life described as a "rat race" and for many people it really is a race. But most people don't see it as a long distance race. They see it as a series of short sprints. They sprint from this job to that or this thing they can't live without to the next thing they can't live without. And when a crisis occurs, they find they have no stamina. They hit the wall and wind up with a faith that is completely out of breath.

Paul reminds us we need patience and endurance. Patience grows from endurance. Endurance comes through the strength God gives us through our faith in Christ. You see, it's really quite simple. It all goes back to Christ and comes from Christ. The more we seek Christ, the more we depend upon Christ. The more time we spend in the presence of Christ, the more strength to endure we are given. And the more strength to endure that we receive, the more patience we develop. We learn to breathe deep of and in the Spirit.

Joyful Thanksgiving

Finally, Paul tells us that we should joyfully give thanks to God in all circumstances.

How are we supposed to be joyfully thankful all the time? Sometimes it's hard enough just being thankful. Sometimes the circumstances of life are such that it seems hard to be thankful for anything, let alone be joyfully thankful. Yet, that's exactly what Paul tells us to be. And again, he starts at the root cause of our thankfulness. That root cause is our relationship with God through Christ. At the heart and center of everything we are and do is God, who through Christ, has transferred us into the Kingdom of God's Son.

As long as we remember that, as long as we stay on board that bus, so to speak, we are assured of our safe arrival and we can and will be filled with joyful thanksgiving.

Somewhere I heard a story about a little boy who was trying out for a part in the school play. He had his heart set on being in it. He didn't care what part he got; he just wanted to be in the play. Mom was afraid he would not be chosen and would come home brokenhearted. On the day they announced the parts, Mom was ready. She waited somewhat nervously and impatiently until her son got off the bus. She watched as he ran to the door filled with excitement. Out of breath, he proudly announced, "Guess what, Mom, guess what? I get to be one of the people who claps and cheers."

In a sense, Paul is saying that we have all been chosen to be the people who clap and cheer. God fills us with God's strength which enables us to endure and develop patience and fills us with the spirit of joyful thanksgiving that allows us to clap and cheer.

Paul's prayer is very powerful. It is a prayer fit for anyone and any church. It is a prayer for God's strength; for endurance and patience and for a spirit of joyful thanksgiving. All of which is possible, Paul says, because we have been "transferred into the kingdom of God's beloved Son through redemption and forgiveness." That's the one thing that undergirds all of this. It begins there and ends there. We have been transferred into God's kingdom through our faith in Christ and that's all we need. God's redemption and forgiveness through Christ covers us, surrounds us, undergirds us, and lifts us up.

Just remember what that bus driver said, "Don't you be getting on any other bus, or you'll get lost."

Rely on God's strength for endurance, patience, and a spirit of joyful thanksgiving.

Lectionary Preaching After Pentecost

The following index will aid the user of this book in matching the correct Sunday with the appropriate text during Pentecost. All texts in this book are from the series for the Second Reading, Revised Common Lectionary. (Note that the ELCA division of Lutheranism is now following the Revised Common Lectionary.) The Lutheran designations indicate days comparable to Sundays on which Revised Common Lectionary Propers or Ordinary Time designations are used.

(Fixed dates do not pertain to Lutheran Lectionary)

Fixed Date Lectionaries *Revised Common (including ELCA)* *and Roman Catholic*	**Lutheran Lectionary** *Lutheran*
The Day of Pentecost	The Day of Pentecost
The Holy Trinity	The Holy Trinity
May 29-June 4 — Proper 4, Ordinary Time 9	Pentecost 2
June 5-11 — Proper 5, Ordinary Time 10	Pentecost 3
June 12-18 — Proper 6, Ordinary Time 11	Pentecost 4
June 19-25 — Proper 7, Ordinary Time 12	Pentecost 5
June 26-July 2 — Proper 8, Ordinary Time 13	Pentecost 6
July 3-9 — Proper 9, Ordinary Time 14	Pentecost 7
July 10-16 — Proper 10, Ordinary Time 15	Pentecost 8
July 17-23 — Proper 11, Ordinary Time 16	Pentecost 9
July 24-30 — Proper 12, Ordinary Time 17	Pentecost 10
July 31-Aug. 6 — Proper 13, Ordinary Time 18	Pentecost 11
Aug. 7-13 — Proper 14, Ordinary Time 19	Pentecost 12
Aug. 14-20 — Proper 15, Ordinary Time 20	Pentecost 13
Aug. 21-27 — Proper 16, Ordinary Time 21	Pentecost 14
Aug. 28-Sept. 3 — Proper 17, Ordinary Time 22	Pentecost 15
Sept. 4-10 — Proper 18, Ordinary Time 23	Pentecost 16
Sept. 11-17 — Proper 19, Ordinary Time 24	Pentecost 17
Sept. 18-24 — Proper 20, Ordinary Time 25	Pentecost 18

Sept. 25-Oct. 1 — Proper 21, Ordinary Time 26	Pentecost 19
Oct. 2-8 — Proper 22, Ordinary Time 27	Pentecost 20
Oct. 9-15 — Proper 23, Ordinary Time 28	Pentecost 21
Oct. 16-22 — Proper 24, Ordinary Time 29	Pentecost 22
Oct. 23-29 — Proper 25, Ordinary Time 30	Pentecost 23
Oct. 30-Nov. 5 — Proper 26, Ordinary Time 31	Pentecost 24
Nov. 6-12 — Proper 27, Ordinary Time 32	Pentecost 25
Nov. 13-19 — Proper 28, Ordinary Time 33	Pentecost 26 Pentecost 27
Nov. 20-26 — Christ the King	Christ the King

Reformation Day (or last Sunday in October) is October 31 (Revised Common, Lutheran)

All Saints' Day (or first Sunday in November) is November 1 (Revised Common, Lutheran, Roman Catholic)

Books In This Cycle C Series

GOSPEL SET
Praying For A Whole New World
Sermons For Advent/Christmas/Epiphany
William G. Carter

Living Vertically
Sermons For Lent/Easter
John N. Brittain

Changing A Paradigm — Or Two
Sermons For Sundays After Pentecost (First Third)
Glenn E. Ludwig

Topsy-Turvy: Living In The Biblical World
Sermons For Sundays After Pentecost (Middle Third)
Thomas A. Renquist

Ten Hits, One Run, Nine Errors
Sermons For Sundays After Pentecost (Last Third)
John E. Berger

FIRST LESSON SET
The Presence In The Promise
Sermons For Advent/Christmas/Epiphany
Harry N. Huxhold

Deformed, Disfigured, And Despised
Sermons For Lent/Easter
Carlyle Fielding Stewart III

Two Kings And Three Prophets For Less Than A Quarter
Sermons For Sundays After Pentecost (First Third)
Robert Leslie Holmes

What If What They Say Is True?
Sermons For Sundays After Pentecost (Middle Third)
John W. Wurster

A Word That Sets Free
Sermons For Sundays After Pentecost (Last Third)
Mark Ellingsen

SECOND LESSON SET
You Have Mail From God!
Sermons For Advent/Christmas/Epiphany
Harold C. Warlick, Jr.

Hope For The Weary Heart
Sermons For Lent/Easter
Henry F. Woodruff

A Hope That Does Not Disappoint
Sermons For Sundays After Pentecost (First Third)
Billy D. Strayhorn

Big Lessons From Little-Known Letters
Sermons For Sundays After Pentecost (Middle Third)
Kirk W. Webster

Don't Forget This!
Robert R. Kopp
Sermons For Sundays After Pentecost (Last Third)

www.ingramcontent.com/pod-product-compliance
Lightning Source LLC
Chambersburg PA
CBHW071739040426
42446CB00012B/2397